THE UNCOVERING

(poems)

by
Jennifer J. Camp

Fernwood
PRESS

The Uncovering
poems
©2024 by Jennifer J. Camp

Fernwood Press
Newberg, Oregon
www.fernwoodpress.com

Printed in the United States of America

Page design: Mareesa Fawver Moss
Cover design: David Ewing

ISBN 978-1-59498-120-3

For my parents, because all the words, you believed every one
And for Justin, who always believes

CONTENTS

WELCOME

Grip the pages softly
let them bend
in your hands
but keep turning
do not be afraid.

Warning

I have spent my life
trying so hard to fill
places in me never
emptied—doubt, distrust
how is there room
for anything else if
this space first is
not cleared.

RECIPE

What if trying to create
beauty happens in
the expectation of its
possibility more than
the striving to pull
coax demand plead
it forth oneself.

RECOGNITION

Coming up for air
means recognition—

you were drowning.

A Request

I ask my heart to break free
to stand, to speak,
unmuted and strong but
it lies paralyzed, stifled
not yet free from breaking.

ARMOR

Words try to hurt me
but this heart wears
armor now.

SAFETY

Little one where did you go
to find protection, a bunker
to hide.

Prescription

Do not be afraid
dear heart
to feel.

QUESTION

Heart, you are
battle-scarred weary
so what can I tell you
what would be kind.

EVIDENCE

She was convinced
she was lost
what can I say
otherwise.

The Story It Tells

Regret does not want
to be silenced.
But don't listen

the road it travels,
bags slung over shoulder,
leather shoes scuffing dirt

is marked by graves,
pockmarked words burying
dead of generations.

Because What If
You Could

Coax them out of hiding
offering kindness
a gentle smile
emotions disguising story
untranslated
misunderstood.

PROMISE

Press sweet
sun-freckled skin against
cheek promising
scars yet to come.

Should we tell her its
coming or stay here
breathing in time and
out hope.

WE'VE ALL HAD ABORTIONS

she said, dark hair, wild and
beautiful puffing out in a
curly tumble behind her
ear, and I heard her clearly
I think, even though I
wasn't sure while the band,
a throw-back to high school
nostalgia, filled the summer air
so it felt thick, hot,
even while a cool breeze
fluttered our skirts and made
me reach for my elbows
instinctively to keep warm.
And I realized she spoke
metaphorically, her eyes flashing
with empathy yet it
felt conspiratorial.
My voice straining to speak for
I understood her discomfort—
her impulse to soothe after I
said the words,
easy-off-the-tongue-jarring-to-the-heart:
sixteen, Christmas vacation, I know
what it means.
It is still strange to get my heart
around what I did. I confess.
Forget connection, relating,
longing to appease
at this party on the patio,
raw tuna on tortilla crisps
and bacon-wrapped figs

passed on platters as I stood,
my blue-gray leather wedges
edged near the swimming pool,
watching water gently push
against blue Mediterranean tile.

WANT

It can be convincing, the argument
that love speaks a language we
can understand. It needles its way in,
a jab of sarcasm, the curl of half-turned
smile, knees on floor, midday,
journals filled with cursive pleas,
a bit of melodrama maybe,
but earnest and sincere all the same
until posturing becomes proof
we make ourselves believe because we
want to
we want to
we want.

ASSURANCE

You don't need to tell me
trying too hard to be loved
will upend all efforts
to be worthy of the exercise.

Proposition

Remain
in sacred space
reserved for
presence not
just memory.

IN THE MISSION

The light is not golden here
pulled in the way I am,
not like it is on clean cotton sheets
warm in morning sunlight
or like pastoral beauty
from that Andrew Wyeth poster,
paper print of breeze blowing
curtains in an open window,
the print I bought in the Philadelphia
art museum shop when I was twenty-six,
rolled up in a cardboard tube and
never puttied to our beige
apartment walls off Rittenhouse Square,
to shine through cracks
in this shuttered window in San Francisco
where my determined hands
scrub soap onto an oil-crusted pan
twenty years and many agreements later
to find the word golden—or even light—
cannot describe nostalgia now,
this golden light on my skin.

THE RELAY

You didn't know your race
would become my own,
this battle with shadows
at the hand-off,
eyes on the baton
and feet thundering ahead
as I run hard, fast,
chase the shadow
you could never catch.
I took the hand-off, accepted it
without question just like you,
held it firm in my hand,
kept up the pace
just like you taught me,
feet aching from a speed I could
never match until I fell,
knees bloody and staggered
limbs aching as I
took off my shoes
(where are you?)
flexed toes in cool grass
and lay myself down.

WHAT YOU SAY

There are many
kinds of bravery you say
and I recognize
the one kind
required for
two women
—sisters, they say,
in folding chairs
makeshift church pews
and across
kitchen counters
fingers curled around
steaming cups
of coffee
to let their eyes
hold one another
in confession:
I hear you
I love you
and I will stay.

How It Is

There is no
excuse, well,
it is impossible:
life lacking
risk and
adventure.

In the Creek

We adventured
to a land
we'd never been
but fully knew
arms swinging
at our sides
down the back steps
the dogs running
at our heels
through orchard
canopied with branches
already since budded
and filled with
tired green leaves
to find mystery
perfect treachery
maybe lions, tigers
and bears
or at least a
dry creek bed
requiring
walking sticks
that will do no good
against rattlesnakes,
twisted ankles and poison oak.
But no matter.
We were never

returning anyway—
the beautiful impact
of life
stepping
one foot at a
time out the door.

THE TRUTH IS

I looked for you
to fill
the holes in me
—blamed you
for not having
the tools to fill them.
I am sorry.

When I Pick It Up

I worry that life's rhythm,
its long arm extended,

inviting me to pick up
my instrument,

will be one I don't recognize
and know

how to play
with distinction

and beauty
and not the clanging gong.

BATTLEGROUND

I can trust this mind. It does its best
to piece together the heart's
general confusion, a malady of

distrusting love and beauty's
general incompleteness.
Wanting lack and then begging

flawed decision (to agree with
what breaks it rather than what
mends it). Their arguments upend me.

I don't know what is good bad,
left right, up down, and the
tumbling leaves me breathless.

Desire's death: I need this war to stop.

To Argue With the Self

I will continue to make you
uncomfortable
bent-over
pressing into dark
attic corners stacked
with boxes taped
and closed tight,
layers of words and doubts
ripping open the corners
tearing free the flaps
clamped shut
to pull out this story,
the one where you
believed words you said
held meaning and magic
a child with power to
retrieve, to set free
any dream packed and buried
from loss and lies.

VALLEY FLOOR

Twisted smoke
the remains of
this house
filled with hordes
dressed as beauty.
I drip angst
and insecurity
until I am surely
suffocating.
This excess
of striving
removing
all warmth
from the room.
I am convinced
something in me is
missing
rather than the other
way around.

THE BOOK

I will mark the place, soft-run my palm
flat on the cover's surface,
faded blue linen, thick vanilla cream.

Black typed letters either singing or
whispering a landscape with feigned
beginning, middle and end. Like my life

when I turn it on its side, aching for the
most beautiful pages scented with pine
from Yosemite—and California almond blossoms

thick with bloom. Buzzing bees drink nectar
from gentle stems, and I am heavy with story,
use a single paragraph to describe the warmth of golden

sun on my skin, walk barefoot down
orchard rows of harvest, pick hot nuts off the ground.
Feel this shell, smooth and round in my hand.

I crack it open, popping tender sweetness in my mouth,
enjoy the fast-forwarding, this life,
pollination to birth to death, fortifying

the next sentence I am only beginning to read.

IF (LIFE)

Through the oak door
heavy on it hinges
she walks
back muscles strong
and eyes sharp
to observe every detail of this life
stretched out before her
a canvas
with intricate lines and
thick layers of color
clovers and gray wet
sidewalk
ambulance screeching
through intersection
wild horses thundering
in meadows a child
searching for home
and an eldery man trying
to lift one leg
into
his trousers
the muscles straining
as he moves
and the girl turns
the ache of longing
too great
how life
surely bursts
out from itself
an explosion of
determination and
unmet desire.

FINDING PLACE

How do I explain I am not alone even here
both younger and wiser with time's passing
as my mind imagines you
set free from rules and all that
makes sense, to let sense experience
what is beyond and (perhaps, this is most true)
the heart's exploding from the weight of
a simple I love you, the spirit lifting to meet
yours where we have

always belonged.

TRINITY: WHAT COMES AROUND

What does it take to find you
she asks, and I don't know if
I can say this most powerful truth
in such plain language, but
it is the only way I can say it:
let them love you;
let yourself be loved.

THE SORTING

Who is to know if dreams can be trusted
the ones that fill our minds
with thoughts and images too confusing
to sort out,
a kaleidoscope of fragmented
color texture and sound
pulling us this way and
that so we are dizzy,
unmoved and adrift from
what we thought we knew
except we sort the pieces, we remember
a moment here and there that
feels weighty,
imposing upon
reason and memory until what
was down is now up,
making us question what we know
is true
from what
is false,
soaring emotion and opinion
until truth extracts itself from
the mess,
straightens its shirt,
rumpled from the chaos
and does a cartwheel,
smiling endearingly
and asking you to follow.

THE CHOICE

Nothing is more satisfying than stretching
arm overhead
back lengthening
toes and limbs reaching
for air and
wondering how much farther
can we go
if this feels so wonderful
the awakening of senses long
deadened
from playing it safe.

September Morning

It is easy to imagine ocean here
the cracking like glass breaking
in violence beyond me in me
even in stillness
its imagined peace disquieting me
with its offer to usher in
any sound
or memory
or vision impossible
otherwise to know
when the sun lights the sky
breaking open
one at a time
like bright angels of stained glass
not yet illumined but offering
intricate beauty all the same
as I sit here in the early hours
by candlelight and
a train in the distance signals its warning blast
and the rumble of its rails
reverberates miles away to my room
where above me a jet engine pierces
the still morning
joining sky earth ocean
to pull me in to the sounds within me
and its disruption to the morning
I ache to soothe
but can't when disquiet is not
only outside but within.

SUNDAY AFTERNOON

We sit outside on blue picnic benches,
feet in the dirt under
an umbrella-ed patio
drinking pints of beer and writing with
earpods in our ears.
We wear our reading glasses,
your two-toned brown and blue,
mine black, and it is a memory tucked away
that reminds me
of our dreams to compete
and achieve and
measure ourselves by
happiness that comes
with the kind of success
you can hold in
your hands rather than
the kind I ache to describe to you now,
a bumbling falling and knowing
less in my head
and more in my heart
to conceive
anything is possible.

THE PLEA

Even running in what seems like circles
can make you stronger than
staying frozen
reluctant to take any risk
for fear of falling.

THE EXCHANGE

He leans across the dining table
elbows pressed underneath
shoulders that have carried
on them many journeys
you have carried him for many journeys
and he says it is literal
your love is literal
that you are love
and when you love we
are unforgetting
all so easily forgotten
a literal love
manifest here
here now
how he touches you.

DREAM

I dream often I am unable to run
my arms pumping
my knees raised high one after the other
and I am going nowhere
it is the worst feeling
my chest tightens thinking of it now
from my desk
dark blanketing my shoulders
before dawn raises the velvet curtain of day
for I am desperate to move forward
terrified of immobility
paralysis
stuck in one place
with my body not cooperating with my mind
so I am slogging
through sand that presses against
all muscles
all self-propulsion forward
and I have never felt
more powerless
breathless
and mute
from the effort.

BLAZE

In photographs my mother
wears a red tube top
blue denim skirt
wrapped around her waist
her eyes wet and bright and
crinkled at the corners
her lips pursing with
the edges hinting up
and I see beyond her
the blue sky and orchard
and deep brown of earth
melting to horizon
even as she blazes arm akimbo
a solitary spark unwilling
to fan the flame.

LIE

It breaks open
when we say it,
our words ineptly crashing
through fog
until your truth
carries us forward,
a torch of light on
feelings we
thought were too ugly
to name or claim.
You see, our efforts
to please
sent hearts to play
hide-and-seek
when we had forgotten how
to rescue them at all.

BRAVERY

It is worth it to write it down
corral memory and meaning
so they meet friendly-like
in the same room
reclusive strangers who are
awkward at parties
shirking when approached
in conversation
for hope mesmerizes them
and they freeze with
nothing to say.

ROOM

The crowds stack the stands
a stadium of dominoes
about to topple forward
why is everyone always on the brink of falling
forward backward out of control
a mother holds a child
sleeping in her arms
and teeangers congregate
in overcharged pods of laughter
and taunts where they challenge each other
to set off the firecrackers
they've hidden in jean pockets
to pass the time.
I am unsure what to do with myself
as I make my way through the crowds
rock music and elevated voices
filling the spaces between us
so I grab your hand
always with me
and though I can't see you
I can sense your steps
feel your breath on my neck
knowing your eyes shine
bright in a crowd
ready to catch and hold
what needs holding,
patient in expectation of
chaos breaking and knowing
we will still breathe.

SEND

The human heart can
hold so much

a storm of chaos pushing
against its edges until

it bursts,
emotion wrestling

with memory as it
falls, tumbling,

no sense of up or down
as you catch it

before it breaks
before the impact

you are loved,
you are loved.

INVISIBILITY IS NOT
ANYONE'S SUPERPOWER

She says she is invisible
and watches my face
eyes bright, creases in the corner,
telling a story she feels compelled
to tell, and I wonder if the words
are true (although how can anyone
judge emotion—definitely not as
right wrong good bad)
and anyone speaking the heart's
ache is the beginning of healing,
the rescue from the lie:
you are unseen unnoticed
unimportant unvalued unwanted,
a string of absences until
you begin to believe them and
forget your voice can only be quieted
if you ignore the raging
beating of your heart.

THE EXCHANGE

Who will you tell the whispers to
if not to me,
so I can gather them
like flowers
bouqueted and fragrant,
a stem behind your ear,
and lean in, my breath
becoming yours,
to kiss
your lips
your eyes
your face
and attune
your beating heart
to my rhythm,
this listening
to what
is true.

CARE LABEL

You can try to crush this
heart between your hands
soft and pink, it will
surely give way to you,
a beautiful mess
of muscle and blood and hope,
but what you don't see
is its strength
invisible to you
and how that will never work.

DRIFT

Let me not drift away from you
a piece of heart debris separated
from where it belongs.

THE MIDDLE PLACE

The wonder of a day
cannot be contained,
for it is where you look, she says,
that pulls you toward what you
most love or most hate.
And I can't help you here,
in the middle place of refusing
to look anywhere that makes it
possible for your heart to feel.

Questions for This Lament

He tells me memory is a gift,
a solace for loss, the holding
of moments so the
leaving is less painful.
But I think he means the
beautiful and less terribles ones.
For what holds these moments?
Are they worth less because
they represent pain?
They speak loud, don't they?
And why should we heed such noise?
Maybe it's shame who does it
—her talent to slice through silence,
jarring the space where
happiness makes her home.
We can hear her, down lonely hallways
and streets packed with people,
lonely with wisdom too
great to be ignored.

How It Is

The cries rise up in the day
just like night, but disguised.

Absence of wonder dulls our senses.

MONDAY IN SEPTEMBER

It is the first rain of the season,
kitten paws padding on the roof
in gentle rhythm, and I keep the
windows open though water
splashes the sills and wets
the furniture and floors.
I want morning air
to rush through this
tightly sealed house,
stir my complacent heart
asleep again before dawn.

WHERE IS THE AX
FOR THE BEANSTALK

when fear
the false giant
thunders in
convincing you
that risk-taking
is no more
and there
is more
to lose
than gain.

THE MOTHERS

How can I tell you
the fear of leaving this
landscape both
terrible and kind
when small hands
were pocketed
in our own,
our voices
sang stories
of imaginary bear hunts
and our laps creased
rocking chairs,
soft wisps of air
brushing our cheeks.
The exodus began long ago
before we were ready,
with their car keys in pockets
and backpacks crammed with
devices for learning to leave,
returning but never
to what was.
And together
we push
against the precipice
of beginning
and ending,
leaning wearily
where once
we stood
with confidence,
the map we held
firm in our hands.

AFTER SCHOOL DROP-OFF

The kitchen counter is filled
with photos that show us all together,
quiet memories holding love and risk
and adventures and then that
Ed Sheeran song plays on my phone,
the one about the supermarket flowers
and his grandmother
who died who loved him
and I am a mess of tears
letting myself stay.

WITH NO NET

We hold a grip—tenuous and resolute
on memory, a slippery beauty we know
cannot be contained as
she dodges between flowers and races up
sides of buildings too high to climb,
tumbling like an acrobat from
cloud to cloud until the freefall
—tangling her hair and silencing
laughter that sounds a bit wild
though kind and free.

What Happens Later

The room was spare
one desk, two chairs
by the window. He offered me
a cup of water, my face sweaty from a
mountainous driveway my bike tried to climb,
and fixed his spectacled eyes on mine.
He was so gentle and kind, I knew
I might tell him the truth.
He prayed, the room
holding me into itself, and then words too big
for my tongue tumbled out, doing cartwheels
in a lopsided mess to tell the abbreviated
but well-rehearsed story about my children,
the tiny town I let suffocate me,
and the confusion that came later
when my own hands
would not wash
clean for twenty years
when I began to try.
It's not funny the way
life's absence clings to you,
or the haunting that comes
after life is gone, but
both filled the room even here.
My brow still damp from exertion,
no amount of effort would help ease
their grip except the act of
relaxing into them.
So let them tell the story.
But his eyes, kind and patient,
held mine and I shared with him

my decision in the orchard
to have the abortion at age sixteen
and of the decades of space,
of waiting to feel anything,
of numbing and then
falling into kindness
I will never deserve until
I turned.
Then I took the paper cup
still in my hands
to my mouth and drank,
the water rushing down my throat.

EXPLANATION

He asked me why kindness is a word
I used to describe God, and I tell him
about the falling into vastness—
a freedom and gift of holding nothing
and being held.

THE CONSIDERING

Swallow me up if you must
I am playing games with you anyway
and can't be trusted.

Or So (We're Told)

Who is to say when beauty begins and
ends, certainly not the day he made
you or when all hell broke loose
and we imagined the lilies
intoxicating us, drenched in dew,
their scent permeating thick night air,
where robin's wavering notes from the garden
lamppost unsettle us in our bed,
cotton sheets wrapped around
our feet, books heavy
in ours laps, minds here and
not here in that space of imagining—
the putting together
(or reunification)
of all things broken and hard,
the curses flung like torches
as we fall until
memory turns to singing
and the end of things turns
rightside up and beginning
becomes clear again
or so we're told.

Even One

Stacks of words are underrated
even one can hold the whole world.

Whereabout

I sit in dim light. The room,
a converted garage where we keep
our bikes on the wall and our desks
kissing each other near the bookshelves,
is still, although the Mountain View train
rumbles through a few miles away around six
and my dog will on occasion moan and then sigh
and lick his lips, his teeth clacking together after he yawns,
and then lick himself until I can't block out the sound anymore
and demand that he stop but yet it is still, a stretched out
place where I am convinced the world is far away
and I am in some separate place accessible and
inaccessible even to myself and I work to
find clues as to my whereabouts, pulling
out a slice of memory—an uneasy
wrenching of the heart, but
it is really the present that
both haunts and invites,
the past crowding in,
wanting to be included while the current
moments want to stay untouched and unharmed.
And in the pauses of discussion between the two, a staggering
around like two drunken teenagers wanting to have their way, I let
   the stillness
quiet them, do the work I cannot accomplish on my own and light
a candle, its light flickering in brilliant warm gold while night
blinks open its eyes a bit and eases itself
out of the room.

To Decide

You do not have to be clever
to be true. Already it is so easy
to trick ourselves into regret.
Yet it is the present, holding
the vastness of everything
that makes hope, that meal
we choose whether to eat or
drink, the least complicated
decision we need to make.

BEAUTIFUL TERRIBLE

How do we hold it
the ache of the beautiful terrible
except to unbind its hands
and let it stagger singing and
tripping around the room.

The Exchange

Duplicitous heart, how can you be trusted?
You are called blessed but
how can I believe it, your lies
bringing discord and not mercy,
angst rather than peace, so I surrender
you—you are no longer mine. I reject
my old heart and receive my new one
—a heart soft and good, gentle and strong,
dependable and kind, always kind.

THE DEEPER PLACE

How long can you sit in the silence
believing God does not speak
here, letting doubt, that
rotted blanket, wrap you in
no safety, no warmth.
For in the deeper place he
excavates, telling you many
things that can be trusted.
Watch him make deception,
with muddy face, drag itself
out by the tail.

INSIDE

I forget there is nothing
to lose in me by loving
and everything to gain.

THE RESCUE

It wasn't hard to believe she was out there
poised like an overstuffed circus performer
on the highwire or the girl in the
old black-and-white movies who gets stuck in
a predicament and needs to be saved.
I like to be saved. But the way her eyes
heeded mine and she cried I had to try
to save her. After all, I was brave,
and my mom was in the kitchen
cooking breakfast and wouldn't notice
if I slipped onto the cement ridge outside
the front porch above the tangle of rose bushes
where the cat, crouching and meowing louder
now, stared fixedly at me,
"What are you going to do anyway?"
I liked the dare. One bare foot in front
of the other, I groped forward in inches,
intent on rescue, on completing the mission.
With the rose bush's claws scraping my bare
legs—this went on for what was surely a hundred years
—I stretched to touch her, my fingertips grazing
the gray fluff of fur on her chest and I lost
all semblance of balance and I fell into an embrace
of leaves and thorns, my cotton nightgown
ensnared in the branches, my limbs striped and oozing
red at their punctures. (I must have screamed.)
And my mom, a swirl of brown curls and resolve,
a pair of strong hands reaching down, extricated me
from my trap. And the cat, bored and disturbed
by the commotion, jumped down between
brambles to the soft ground below.

SCRIPTURE

She talks about God a lot
in her poems, a mention
tossed over her shoulder
like she doesn't care—
about him being not-living but
an idea, a spectral, a ghost whose
ambivalence about life
can't penetrate all convictions
like, say, the sharks
in the water who will
eat you or the fluff of clouds
that melt into the stomach of
a city's night air. Because, even
collectively, mystery and beauty
and danger are not enough of a
reason to believe that words are
one of two things: something
you either consume or monsters
you let swallow you whole.

Risk

She tests the waters first before
she jumps, twisting like barbed wire,
one arm sticking out for balance while
she dips in one toe. I don't believe
she will jump. She is too afraid of the mess
of untangling herself upon landing.

MOTHER AT NIGHT

Night shakes open her blanket upon
the grass, the forest, the houses
and invites us to sit with her.
From her basket she retrieves the moon,
stars twinkling in merry laughter,
spreading her arms wide,
an invitation to open our mouths
and sing. The crickets she beckons first,
their spindles reverberating off
back porches and under canopies
of trees until the frogs join in
and the jazz singer of the night,
the nightingale, shows off
in chugs of improv: "This is how
you sing like you're made to."
So she cover us, pulls us to her,
and we inhale her sweetness—
dew upon the grass, our faces,
our toes, opening our mouths
to drink in the sky, the earth,
the grass, the air and then
listen to the stars singing,
singing us to sleep.

WILD HORSES

I assemble my thoughts before
she asks the questions, corralling
them like stallions wild and
skittish, determined to stay free.
I want to know them,
deeper places of the heart
—unruly, untamed, so prone
to breaking. And the story I
thought I knew isn't real,
held together as it is by
words trying to tell a story
but with no sense of who
and why and how. So how
does one interrogate the past?
I don't know except to
interpret memory as a dream,
holding together the best
it can with emotions neither
good nor bad, roped together
with pain that likes to run
and run and run. And I wonder
at any story's soundness—
how the heart can be trusted
when it is afraid to be quiet
and still.

PALO ALTO BIKE PATH

It is new, our biking everywhere,
bags slung on our backs as we
pump over the railroad tracks
and thread paths with dozens of
kids winding their way to school.
We go too, bending past
the cemetery where Berta,
our next-door neighbor,
lies buried, ducking tree limbs
that need pruning and dodging
old women in pajamas and
headphones who can't hear
our bright warning bells,
which is risky. And I follow
you—you're always willing
to go ahead—watching your
strong back press forward,
pushing down as you lean
over the handlebars. You
know I love the effort
it takes in keeping up.

GRASP

In the letting go I am
holding everything more
tightly now

the memory of you
looking at me
across the room
mouthing I love you

I am in love with you
and everything so beautifully
falling apart.

ON STAYING

You can tell me he didn't build this
and I wouldn't believe you—
light and trees and family and work,
although the manufacturing of truth
and blustering of pride I believe
speaks to deeper whispers
within us—love me love me
I am hurting here, do you care?
And the earth cracks open to
swallow us and cries, and this is
when the mothering begins,
the loving in absence—
our absence—and the housing
of pain to love despite rejection,
denial, the chasing of demons
when his arms, wider than
any mother's, stays breaking
open again and again.

THE WAIT

It's the waiting that's hardest
they will tell you, that
space feeling like nothingness
and yet heaviest all the same.
We are convinced we hate it,
or at least resent it, as if being
tortured by swarms of bees or
falling from a cliff—the
calm of knowing death
is impending, when really
it is not more certain
than this moment now.

How She Begins

She'll jump in every puddle
if you let her, hands held up
like a crazed conductor
prompting music to fly or
the guy at the race starting line,
gun in the air, loving the power
he holds in his hands.
Because for her, beginning includes
the anticipation of motion—
the propelling forward,
feet leaving the earth and
exploding down again so
quickly but defiantly,
each time different than before.

THE RACE

In evening there is exhale
but also examination, although
that is not what I want to do.
I would much rather tell
myself to keep running until
my lungs break free from their
casing and I stagger breathless
and aching to a finish line where,
when I think about it, there is no
cheering or fans waving
their hands wildy or red streamers
or music or water to quench my
scalding throat but desert sand billowing
in pale blue sky and a single
scaled lizard pausing in the sun,
its forked tongue smelling the
air for idols, and I think this will do,
to lay my head down and consider
if this day will end before I stop
refusing to pretend I am okay.

Riding Home

What are the rules for risk taking
I wonder as I pedal down Alameda Street
before it merges into Junipero Serra Boulevard.
It is two-thirty. Cars pile up on
my left, but I've got AirPods in my ears,
and I don't want to merge, move out
into traffic and call attention to myself
like I need to so I don't get bumped
by a car. I need to merge to the left,
move out of this bike line into traffic
but I can't—you see my predicament don't you?
If I don't merge I don't make it home.
I will be stranded, near these narrow bricks
on the side of the road. But this is no yellow brick
road. I am wild and weak and solitary in
this crowd, especially now that I've stopped
on the side of the road where I don't
belong but from where I can't move. And
I stay frozen, where I don't belong,
fiddling with my bike handles and
looking down as if I am in deep thought,
not scared, in case the people in the
cars pulled over at the light look over at me
and wonder what this forty-seven year old
woman is doing pausing (not freaking out).
And the light turns green. Still
I wonder what will get me to move.

OF COURSE YOU

Of course it comforts me to think
we are the same, your blue eyes
a study of my own, where I dive
inside swimming and swimming,
willing to drown to be with you
rather than coming up for air.

COLLECTED (THE MOTHERING)

My mother sent me every poem
I wrote in high school, my handwriting
printed rather than scripted in the
spaghetti cursive my English teacher
hated, "i's" dotted with lollipop circles,
a collection of observations emphatic
and slightly dramatic on wide-ruled,
multi-colored scratch paper, clearly
anything I could find. And I thought
I would hate them, or, at least,
struggle to relate to the girl who
sat in her room, *The Far Side* comics
taped to the brown paneled walls,
door closed, at her desk or her bed
with the Sears cornflower blue-and-tan
quilted bedspread, but I hear her
in me now, her voice echoing in
empty space where she thought
no one was listening, no one would
hear, and I gather her inside me,
for I know how to mother now,
your arms around us as you lean in
close, your daughter collected in the
scattered places to hear every
word we say.

GROWING

I told you I would carry you
over creekbed, rock-strewn and
dangerous, up mountainside
and through thickets of trees.
We pause to hear the birds
calling, and you're convinced
it has nothing to do with you,
the fragrance of the boughs
bending over our heads,
pine-stamped with memories of
hiking into wild places we'd
never been before. The flowers
brush our bare legs as the path
winds to the clearing, and we
feel the water in our throats
before we see it: glacier blue,
daring each other to climb up
to the small cliff overlooking
the water and jump. So I let
you go, set your feet down
where the ground is brown
and damp and sure and you
climb without me, knowing
now it will be okay to fall.

IF I'M HONEST

I want to tell you
breathless and lying
you will be okay.
For it is expected.
And pain without
growth is the worst
kind of death.
But I am not ready
to tell truth at the
expense of duplicity.
It is clear you know
the answer anyway.

SAFE

There are many things I can tell you
if I thought you wanted to hear them.
For the burden on you is misplaced,
judgment before you open your mouth,
self-condemnation as failed protection
against me/you.

Can you hear me? Can she?
I must separate from you to
hear her clearly. No, she won't
be safe then. But who is safe?

Let me gather her, all the parts
and misplaced pieces of me from
various places, beginning with
the girl who ran barefoot in orchards
and hid in her room and promised
God/pleaded to do/be better
than she was. For she must
come home now.

And we are listening, you/me
altogether we lean in and listen to her
for it has been too long
since she considered it safe.

HERE

I am not hiding, I tell myself,
for most words are flimsy structures
that can't bear the weight of glory.

WHERE WE LIVED

They hauled in our home on trucks,
four slices of brown paneled doll house
with imagined furniture inside. It
rumbled toward us on flatbed trailers
down the dirt road soon to be graveled

between acres of almond trees my dad
planted with his bare hands. The dust
billowed behind the tires and settled on
the next door neighbor's branches
heavy with harvest. My dad stood

waiting in front of the gray Ford pickup,
his arms thick and sunburnt, directing the
drivers to the cement foundation
where we'd been riding our Schwinns
in circles for weeks waiting for home.

This wasn't the story I told the counselor
when she asked me about where I grew up,
the magic of a house being pulled up a
country road and snapped together
like legos, a house bigger than I had ever seen

where mom let us cartwheel in the living room
with the thick brown carpet and
the big windows looking out into the
wonderland of dirt and grass and trees.
I didn't tell her about our hands

pressing into wet cement around the
base of the TV antennae, index fingers
sketching our names and stick figures
with smiles, or the star thistles scraping
our bare legs as we ran with the dogs
—or the cats we took to the tractor
shed to play house or the swingset
Dad built from the kit from Sears.

She could tell I didn't want to tell
the stories, the making mud cakes
in our underwear or helping change
the sprinklers in the summer and
riding the pipe trailer while we posed
like acrobats bouncing and swinging
from the sides. Instead, what I told her
was described in a few sentences,

terse and to the point: we lived
in the country; our house was a mobile
home; my dad was a farmer. And she
acted like my voice caught in my throat
when I said it. You sound embarrassed,
she said. Are you embarrassed?

And I realize I'm not sure what she
meant or what she heard in my voice
to make her question sound
so accusing and so sad.

SADNESS

I underestimate
what love can hold
and forget it matters.

I Don't Call My Brother

I don't call my brother
on his birthday
or even text—
no card, no cake,

no stretching out
across the great divide

of years and time and space
as if I could shorten it,

as if I could pull it
like a loose
thread on a sweater
and watch it
unravel:

stitches wandering
every which
way to get to
his heart.

ACHING

The air in this room hangs
heavy in agreement

how time seems to linger then
scamper away with our breath.

I am preoccupied with it,
want to coax it to relax into
me, or at least cuddle close
on the coach as we sit in the dark,

my feet bare and cold on the
cement floor. But it is too heavy,
wrapping around an arm and
inviting us to sit awhile, share

some coffee or tea. But I don't
want to hear this, how time
must be shared. I want it all
to myself you see, and then,

perhaps, invite you to come over
and celebrate its passing,
one death and then another
on my terms, not yours.

For there is surely not enough
of it (I am convinced)
to make me live unafraid of
losing what was never mine to keep.

THE COVERING

He tells me he covers me in all ways
in all capacities,

and I think about
what it means to be covered,

making my heart beat both fast
and slow. For it is a hiding place—
unreachable by efforts to strive
or arguments that I am not enough.

All is quieted as I snuggle in,
a little girl with my knees tucked
close to my chest and then braver,
arms released at my sides,

held down by nothing so that
even here, in the covering,
I know now how to step out and fly.

CHOOSE

It is not power we are after
I am convinced.

Yet love feels too costly,
and we choose nothing

as a compromise until it
swallows us up whole.

BELIEVE

There are mornings I awake
unthinking and these are the best

days, my breath speaking to my heart
you are loved, you are okay.

TATTOO

It is in the dark, where you feel
you can't see, but I come to you

here, in shadow places and dimly lit
corners, in the spaces where air is

thin, hollowed out moments with razor sharp
teeth, weapons of war strapped to your

back when yielding isn't an option
to give you

my hand, every crease of my
palm pressed into yours.

Exposed

We hear of shadow places and
become afraid (after all, we can't see them)
and this isn't good so we go deeper

into the recesses of thought, of memory.
holding captive anything that brings
to question how we think, speak, move

as if our own mind's vision will
protect us against infirmity and
all else we imagine to bring harm. But

it is in the shadows where light shines
most brilliant, a contrasting beacon
slicing through the lies we tell so

nothing stays hidden, not
fear, not even the heart.

All That Is

The brick looks strong enough,
stacked white and high, to hold me.
I am at the top of steep gray stairs
and can see people walking
in clumps of one, two and three.

A few carry packagers, a monotone
wash of muted gray on fogged glass.
My breath leaves condensation
on the window. The people walk
away to various places. I wonder
why I watch and why I care.

Except the walls hold no
color here, their silence not a
blanket that shields and protects
but a void, an absence of red
and blue, amethyst and green.

It is too bright and too cold.

I want to feel pain, feel something,
breath blowing on my neck, a
stabbing through my chest,
hunger. But nothing. And that

is what worries me most.

FEELINGS

In the hollowed out places
where something is missing

I search, but my heart fails me,
a cavern reverberating with

the sound of my footsteps as I
tread, hand first at my sides, then

outstretched, my fingers hungry
to touch this blanketed space.

But I can see well enough:
there is nothing here.

On the Plea to Wake Up

When death comes
I want to feel everything
I was afraid to feel while

I was living, my heart
a wild horse's leap from
cliff to waterfall,

this mad froth of body
not crushed by rock but
embraced.

Measuring

It was too small I would say
when asked about where I grew up,
crowded in ways I couldn't handle,
with dirt billowing behind pickups
as farmers rested their forearms
in rolled down windows and drove
down the tree rows checking for leaks
in the water pipes. I would see them
later at the gas station food counter
and serve them ice tea in tall plastic tumblers
and endless cups of bad coffee in chipped
white mugs with brown stripes. They would
talk about weather and crops and politics,
their eyes creased and kind. I never knew to make
a fresh pot of coffee, and they never complained.
I feel bad about that now—that,
and my planning for ways to get out,
stealing looks out the plate-glass window
to Main Street and watching for any
teenage boys to drive by. This
little town that did its best to raise me
—in swimming pools and barefeet and
fireworks, ferris wheels and pickups,
in creeks and star thistles and poison oak,
and the ache of families striving
to make a living on too few acres.
And kids mismeasuring their
roles in a dying town.

WHATEVER IT TAKES

Come close now, do not be afraid.
And I tell him I could never be afraid
with you. So words he coaxes
out of hiding peek out from behind doors,
arms akimbo, hips jutting to the side with sass
and attitude (ready to wrestle me to the ground
if they have to, do whatever it takes)
to tell his stories.

THE IN BETWEEN

It is faulty thinking we tell ourselves
when we can't locate the map required to traverse
these rocky paths of argument that aren't arguments
but failures to connect, a journey more precarious
and necessary in these passing years, when finding
our way back feels a burden too heavy to carry
—and the way forward offers no promises
that things will be okay.

CHILDHOOD

I would like to tell you this is easy
the remembering her name
how sunlight splits open the sky

spilling yellow laughter upon concrete
where our feet, toughened by heat
and play, did not tread softly.

Even now we stumble, eyes turned up-
ward, wondering what to call her,
song thick on our tongues, until light's

hands fold around ours and we follow
her steps, golden splashing upon our
cheeks our arms, our hair,

and she dances out of the shadows
that dimmed our vision and left light
untended to fade.

911

I try to tell you it will be okay
heart beating without air

but there are no promises
to hold except one:

this will end

fighting or surrendering,
hiding or running,

and what is there to do
when all these choices feel the same

but take one breath and another;
dear heart, breathe.

AIR

My greatest fear is drowning
—or asphyxiation, the air pressed
from every place whole and good,
a flat peace, texture gone,
where there is no room for me
and I must settle and sink instead
of struggling like I still do, for air.

INFLUENCE

Clouds bunch together
like overstuffed sheep so
I press my palms
into damp earth and
lie on my back and pretend
to train them. They need

to know the best way
to drift and pattern asphalt
where children play
kickball and hot lava.
I am no shepherd but,
perhaps, a magician

with power to distract
and mesmerize, believe
observation of time and
matter brings meaning when
still I want

more than anything
to control all
—just, everything
around me,

as if rain will fall
where I say and clouds
heed my voice when I speak.

Everything

We played King of the Mountain in the compost pile,
a mound of moist brown steaming in summer sun.
Our mom couldn't see us from the window so

we tested our strength, how hard we could shove
each other off without losing our footing and
tumbling ourselves down.

The strategy was simple: hold your ground,
keep your legs locked, press your palms into
the shoulders of our foes, avoid the Hot Wheels
and toy tractors half-hidden in the battleground
—as well as the tricycle, the get-away vehicle
pushed up to the top in case of emergency surrender.

Hot dirt in everyone's ears and nose and hair.

It was the age of power and authority,
the age of conviction, childish and perfect
when the moment, what we were doing,
was everything: the struggle to exert strength
taintless and pure,

our bare toes plunging deep
into the rim of the top of the world without our knees

even once touching the ground.

HOLDING

Don't tell me my feelings matter
unless you help me hold them

as if, holding them to your chest,
they were your own babies

soothed by mother's heartbeat,
her voice, her smell. Sing them down

from where they want to run,
convinced they are imprisoned and

not free to wiggle and moan and scream.

CARDS ON THE TABLE

I will tell you I am not afraid
of trying because

that is what I am
supposed to say,

and that part is true
—the trying part, but not

the failing. It's the
failing I'm not okay with,

and your knowing
about it, I think, is

the hardest, though
I wonder if that

is true, for
I am most dangerous

when trying to
forgive and

love my
-self despite

you, despite what
I've done or will

do next. But
I want

no one
to know this either.

Almost Happiness

(inspired by Robert Hass's "Happiness")

Because this morning I sit wrapped in
darkness with the ticking clock beating
and the air is still, no outside breeze or even

the sound of trains rumbling on the tracks,
and because I have yet to wake her with
a kiss upon her cheek, soft and hot against mine,

I wonder about sunlight tiptoeing across
the earth with a gentle step like a mother
leaning over the bedside of a beloved daughter,

the whisper of good morning in her ear
—how kind and wonderful
to be coaxed into waking, with pink

sky and golden tipped petals from flowers
stretching for light's kisses too—
and because it shines on me where I look,

I lean back my head and write these words,
eyes closed: she is leaving soon, this October
day, and my heart aches from the missing.

WHEN SHE SINGS

I hear her voice
in my body
the way a child knows it mother
when it is born
her guttural cries pulling forth
all pain all desperation all promise
everything within her
so nothing is not singing
with her
nothing is left behind
and I want to both fold back into her
and burst forth my own song
from a place she built
before any words were formed.

Pain

I am less mean now when I fight,
less of a dog
growling and snapping
as it backs uncomfortably into
a corner but
I still want to bare my
teeth at you,
let you know I am
the one
in control really,
even though I hurt
you, even though I
am wrong.

When I Meet Her

She is beautiful with the light
behind her shining, I
can only see her

silhouette holding
my hand, the two of us
holding hands like we

had never been separated,
never seen death
tearing her

from my womb
without asking her
what she thought or

if she would
rather stay
and still

she holds me—
holds onto me like
love remains and I

am surely falling when
she turns
her face to me.

MEND

The healing comes in fits and starts
and I am not complete

a paper doll cut from thrown-away scraps
—reshaped, recut, repurposed, renewed:

wild outside the lines.

Fold me bend me
watch me tear and
mend,

edges soft and
beautifully flawed.

What Is Good Anyway?

She'll tell you her mind is hollow
her thoughts voiceless, an empty room,
but I hear her,

shout at her, plead for her to feel
compassion,
wake to this wild beautiful

life. Yet she refuses, stays
complacent, one eye
half-open for

life muted, convinced
she has nothing good
to say.

SMALL

Little girl clutches
her metal lunchbox
armed for battle,
waiting for the school
bus to grind and roar
toward her,
swallowing her whole.
She sits in the front seat
to the right of the driver
until the bus is empty and
Willy uncoils his tall body
from the wide wheel,
pale blue eyes fixed on her,
and asks her where she lives,
if she knows her way home.
With no idea how she got here
or how to get back, she stares
at him, voiceless and small,
smaller than she ever knew.
Until he takes her back—
lumbering and bouncing
over potholed country roads,
—back to the school where
her mom waits, eyes filled
with happy tears, to
take her home
take her home
take her home.

SAPPHIRE

I will fight for you
your heart wild and strong
until you believe it
the voiceless singing out
loud and free.

BIRTHING PLAN

You tell me you'll rewrite the landscape one day,
one day all the suffering mended,
one day all the weak made strong,

and I wonder what I will
look like, what beauty looks like,
when love breaks through all pride

in me and I have no cave where I
can hide. Will I stand then
like I do now, brittle and unwieldy,

decay's stench filling the room?
Will you destroy me from the inside out?
Will fire burn me, all of me, so there's nothing left?

Will you plant me, this one seed, deep
in the dirt, birth me from the ashes?

How else does glory sing praise and
what is dead made brand new?

How to Plant a Garden

To tell you what I see would break you
which you tell me you want

not strength, not glory
not self
-reliance, certainly not
self-righteousness

but breaking

the core of bitterness,
the core of contempt for

you, and so

here,

let me tell the ground
breaking
breaking open
the hardened soil

my hands moving the earth
fingers pressing,
voice massaging
      the hard places until
only malleable,
nutrient rich soil
remains

and you, you are ready,
ready for me
to plant a garden within

you, my hands upon
your face so you see me,
hear me, for the
first time:

this is how love grows deep and wide,
covering the whole earth, the continued choice
to stay
like this
for love to grow and grow.

BEAUTY

I have no language for her
to sing as she walks,
autumn gold lacing her hair

like a crown, where time
and season do not wither
her spirit nor discourage her

hips' sway. She is timeless,
floating in mystery she has no
need to explain and kisses

me with soft lips, one eye and
then another until I see me—
like I'm in a movie—abandoning

this twisted place of sabotage
to enter what is inside out:

belief in what is real rather
than in what is readily seen.

WONDER

It is too much
to feel this place

the inhabiting of
love's masterpiece

heaven come down
upon the earth and

I can scarcely breathe
from the wonder of it.

My Friend

Someday, someday I will see
you as I sit here

books piled upon my lap
as if I can read a word

of meaning, affix understanding
in my heart that counts for

more than knowledge but
recognition of our sameness,

glory that you are.

DIRECTION

To lay myself down in this hollow place
filled with nothing but air, puffed full
of time and dreams,

to lay myself down with my eyes
open and clear, let my chest rise and
fall until I draw inward and am

in it—the space of nothingness and everything,
beyond time and space and duty and opinion.

Let us be wild and reckless here,
children running in wide open
fields, toppling over our own

feet as we lose our
balance and you
find your way
to me.

FOLLY OF INTERPRETATION

We do our best to interpret
what we don't understand
chewed up gum flattened into
the sidewalk, a deflated ball abandoned
on the playground, our bodies
wrinkling with age, a family giving up
connecting around the dinner table,
and we create our own stories
around objects and people and
discarded moments to piece together
meaning, always meaning, as if we
have the tools to comprehend our choices
for these fickle and mostly
beautiful hearts.

The Unbelief

We are too beautiful to name it,
the deep place of beauty—

but drape it over ourselves,
play dress-up like in the
silks at Goodwill.

It is not ours, not mine,
not yours, we say,
looking around,
pleading for someone to contradict us.

Meanwhile we look for the next accessory
to doubt our worth.

How we deprecate ourselves
and call it humble,
how we minimize our strength
and call it justified.

How we tear
ourselves apart,
discarded remnants
unwilling to be quilted together even

in patterns like wild ocean and baby fingers and
white feathers floating in clouded sky.

How we wonder why we struggle to believe
we are loved when it is just
a word, the beginning of everything

rejected and sought
with our whole lives to earn and
die for and prove.

FIVE YEARS OLD

Watch me defy you, sweet girl.
You are more than what you believe.

Stand up, lift your face.
I am exhausted by what you carry.
And yet hear: listen to what has taken me
my whole life with you to say.

This voice: unmuted, strong,
a sapphire held to the sun,
sings life now to the heart
you discarded, an injured bird with wings
you were sure could never fly.

I will show you how to love yourself,
how to marvel at beauty,
feathers sprouting from dirt and ash.

Fly now! fly! Wings outstretched,
eyes open, a wild jewel beaming
as you soar brave and untamed
in bright blaze of sky.

SLEEP STATE

It is too easy
to dismiss the miracle of you,
the way you pull a brush through your hair,
the habitual thinking about your day

and stirring in the night—
lying surrendered in your bed
for hours or wandering about the house
waiting for dawn.

You, a miracle realized through
dream and breath and words and dust
are both invitation and kiss
upon lips who love you:

arise and wake or
stay, your life asleep.

ARRESTED

I will sit, paper in my lap
and wait with you
wool blanket shrugged over shoulders
and bare feet pressed to concrete floor.
I am cold, though
impending winter
in California
can be subtle,
a gentle tiptoe in morning
darkness, and I wonder

how you fill every space
and we don't see you,
the miracle of a day,
dawn rising like ocean
tide over dry land and how
I am held here,

in this space beyond this
space and I
let my breath stay
though I am hungry to leave it,

not work so hard
to search for you

in every blade of grass
curled ribbon, smell of
fish over open fire,
every song belted under stars
and on broken bed springs

because every movement,
every cry, is your name
tattooed on my bones.

OCTOBER MORNING

Perhaps there is nothing else
to search for
this trying to find meaning
in every little thing.

I lift my head and darkness
and light melt
together, gray sky
silhouetting the bamboo
so they play a game of tag
—on the roses and the chairs,
on the gravel, on the overhead
bulbs strung like starred necklaces in the sky.

And I wait for something dramatic
to happen—wind whipping the branches
into conversation maybe,
or squirrels acrobating from the trees
to the roof. But it is
still,

a funny thing how the mind
and heart ache
to speak.

YOU ARE WONDROUS AND I AM BEAUTIFUL

What meaning is there in definition?
A sorting, a ranking one moment as memorable and
another as forgettable?
There is so much I do not understand and
I think
I am okay with that—
but even here
I judge myself and grow
uncomfortable, my limited capacity
to dream without boundaries
a world where love is an absolute
and nothing is rank and file.
But you are wondrous and I am
beautiful and together we
inhabit space without time and
measurement, these bodies capable
now of all impossible feats:
climbing mountains without rope,
flying like birds without fear
looking into each other's eyes
and not comparing the shade of your green
to my blue, waiting for eternity to begin
in a way that makes sense for us,
the qualification of meaning
thrown blazing into fire.

WHATEVER IT TAKES

Let me care less about beauty
and more about truth
the ache of the heavens for the sake of love
bringing rescue for the one who is lost
giving hope to the one who is hopeless
fixing all that is broken
all that we've broken
and giving back what was stolen
when we forgot truth,
Love walking around in a garden,
playing hide and seek,
whatever it takes,
to find the objects of affection,
of sacrifice,
of the reason behind all love.

THE LIAR

In the camper parked
out front we played
house. I forget who
was the mom and who
was the dad but
I remember
we fought,
our six-year-old skinny
arms wrapping
around necks
until my
fingernails dug in-
to your flesh,
red blood
polka-dotting
the thin white
underside of your
arms, and when your
mom interrogated
me, blue eyes
squinting and flashing,
I didn't even consider
telling the truth.
I wasn't good at
lying yet, not
able to explain
with any glimmer of
reason the tears
of a six-year-old
girl and the clawed up
tracks on her arms.

JOY

I imagine the ease of having
a best friend
no second-guessing affections or
playing games of
duplicity
but knowing
without judgment
each other's faults,
no sitting across from one another
in an organized circle
but you leaning, leaning up against
me, hand wrapped
up in mine and we would
know all
the secrets,
each other's funny habits,
no hiding or pretending
or worrying what love will require.
It will be like
breathing,
the way we love
without thinking
just life and death—
oxygen filling our lungs.

WEIGHT TO CARRY

Moving toward you,
I think,
is where I am headed
although my feet,
mindless rebellious
things, drag themselves
as if surely twenty
pound weights
cling to their soles
and I tell you
I am afraid—and
though my pen wants
to write down
all my failings for you
to see, like sharing
them will connect us,
warm your
heart to me
so the distance
between us is manageable,
I will not
condemn myself
even if the act of self-derision
makes me look humble
and you would like me.
For, actually, this is it:
the dream of
loving myself
is the greatest
weight I carry
and I struggle
to shake it off.

EMERGENCE

Wash over me until
I can no longer be seen
covered in gray mist
draped around
my shoulders
and adorning my hair.

I will see and not understand
you, your ease of being
delighted in, with
sunlight bright
on your face. I want to
stand there with you

where I am welcome too—
my way of walking,
arms swinging at my side,
an expression of
unselfconsciousness.

Can I forget myself
to be myself?
Let the mist covering
me be a cape billowing
behind me so it looks like
I am walking in clouds

to join you,
making the sky more
beautiful, a palette
of texture and
life bursting out,
eager to be born.

BACK TO MYSELF

Here she is, I've been waiting
for her to show up,
raise my head and see her as
nothing more and more than everything
I've ever dreamed. A lifetime

of rejecting her and still she stands,
hands on hips, a flash of smile,
so
I stand too.
Crossing the

room until there is no space between us
and I melt into her arms,
the realization bitter and cruel:
how desperately I missed her, how desperately
I missed home.

WORKING BACKSTAGE CREW
OF PETER PAN

I watch them
how they do it
in a space all
their own while
present,
bodies swaying to
every note of music
in their heads.

Residency Requirements

I wish I could describe to you the lack of ease
I feel being me, the oscillation between
self-condemnation and feeling nothing at all.

How the freedom of self-forgetfulness would be
the greatest joy—to feel at home, not assessing this
jumble of rooms for need of restructuring,

the soundness of the walls, the arrangement of
the furniture. I want to be happy with how I am,
believe I am a place people want to be.

Joining me for a coffee, talking about nothing
important because of how, by myself, I am loved.
But it is lonely here, the spaces within me

empty, with visitors invited in for only a little
while until I grow uncomfortable with them/me
and ask them to leave, not by saying it outright,

of course, but in my assuming the space
is inhospitable: unsuited for enjoyment,
for entertainment, or for long-term stay.

TIME

Across the landscape is no border
I can see for time is kind,
not a tyrant of fear, beckoning
me to stretch out into its arms (measureless and
dauntless in capacity)
to love backward and forward and sideways
and around me until I am covered.
And work and rest feel different now:
limitless and beautiful in all possibility
for all is here and I am here and you are
here and everything is perfectly beyond
my grasp.

The Unfurling

Don't unwrap yourself around me
though I forget you are here
behind and before, high and low,
covering me when I would otherwise
surely break
the day I sat outside the church,
concrete bench for pew,
red leaves at my feet, and
listened
for your breath, your words,
though you were closer
than any syllables,
than any sound becoming
meaning
for this is how you hold me,
my ear to your mouth,
listening to the air passing
from your lungs to your lips and
into me, your breath my breath,
my lungs expanding with each
exhale of yours.

WHAT CAN I SAY

The prayers broke me open
despite my resistance
the part of me standing
sentry against love.

DAUGHTER

She lets me kiss her each morning,
intoxicating my lips,

making my soul jump
acrobatically around the room,

in this tangled mess
of warmth and goodness

burrowed under blankets
where she holds out her arms,

eyes still squeezed resolutely shut,
to let me fall into them and

enter everything
fleeting and gentle

and beautiful
in its innocence and sweetness

—oh, she is sweet,
and this moment is sweet

and I tumble into it
and let it hold me,

her folding me into what is
good and kind, all that

I don't deserve.

SKY SONG

I lost my breath right there,
legs pumping hard in pedals
—although that wasn't the reason.

It was the arching of oak branches
all the way from heaven to ground.
So I bow with them, sky and tree

and girl while wind shakes
gold leaves
fluttering like paper jewels
to litter the ground

where I ride
inhaling and exhaling glory
thick with anticipation.

WHITE FLAG

I read books about Sabbath keeping
the recalibrating our hearts so they find

their rhythm of rest in you, and it feels like
the ultimate battle I lose daily, throwing

up my white flag and saying this is enough,
I am enough, and I wonder if I will

learn how to stop my war against
time, drape her around my neck

and shoulders like a blanket on a cold
morning and let her whisper, her

warmth pulling me to this earth:
there is no enemy here.

HUMMINGBIRD

I wonder if I am the only one
who sees it. The fluttering of
wings holding her up, the
effort (resolve) to keep
moving. It takes
everything not to sink,
grounded to earth and
time rather than living
in space where measurements
—youth and wisdom, effort
and success—are meaningless,
unfounded. Yet is it, I
could tell her, the upended
effort of living in the future while
running from the past,
ignoring it with all
its sharp edges and predictable
pain that make the present
intolerable, that will help her settle,
breathe deeply again.
But she won't hear it,
the noise of her own wings beating hard
and fast, drowning out all
voices, all help, for she
must find saving, she is
convinced, in her own
movement, the sound of her
own breath and beating
heart voiceless in the wind.

WHAT TO CALL A CIRCLE OF FRIENDS

I tell them of our separateness
as if they didn't already feel it from me,
the choosing to look
at our differences more than
what makes us the same.
But why must I do even that?
Catalogue people—their characteristics
and attitudes, movements and
philosophies as same or
different from me? Right
there I am pushing my way
apart from humanity, like
I don't deserve to be here,
among a crowd of individuals
I must practice considering
my brothers and sisters,
not my enemies.
How might I find my way
to you if I struggle to accept myself?

TELL ME

How might we
choose each step
carefully

while letting this
wildness
in us sing?

MISCALCULATION

I am more than the measurements
of me, a list of accomplishments,
characteristics and moods.
But why must I say I am
more? How can I be less
than I am? Shall I reject
measurements all together?
Maybe that is where I will
begin—
to get to know and
accept neither more
nor less about
me me me.

This Can Hurt

I wander
a child in sparse land
hands empty at my sides
where I am small and
unhurried yet unable to run or,
with abandon, play. This is
the accustomed rhythm,
how shame presses heavy
on my body, my mind—
both molded to the earth
while they are designed to fly.

How might I move here
unencumbered,
no weight upon me,
shackles removed except by
the earth (who hates
me, wants distraction and
disappointed days to rule)?

Convince me otherwise:
I am nothing, not dearly loved,
definitely not loved.

WILD AND FREE

My thoughts disturbed by dog's

feet tapping on kitchen floor,

afraid to come near me and

the fire, an uncertain entity of

heat and flame, while I count

my breaths, my chest rising and

falling to bring awareness of

my mental state, thinking this

will be a pathway to peace but

it stops there, my mind

resistant to movement

not wild like the fire,

eager to run unencumbered

and free.

LAY ME DOWN

Dreams full of speculation
about the reason a man, alone
in a room, leans over the
bed of a sleeping girl and
licks her face as if he were
a dog and she a piece of meat
or why a man, palms nervous,
sweat dripping down his face, becomes
trapped in an elevator, or so he thinks
when it pauses
between two floors for five
seconds before opening its door
at floor eight to let him out,
and then a teacher, young and insecure,
fails to locate her classroom
of pupils, until she does, and
they all laugh at her, derision filling
the room as it spins and swells
and pushes her out
—we do not belong/here
where hearts cannot be trusted
and our confusion leads to
shame. I take each of these thoughts
—the men, the girl, the teacher,
the students, and I let my
heart feel its panic, its
revulsion at a world of strangeness
too much and not enough
and we, its children, tear about
like wild orphans needing
companionship, discipline, and love
and a place to weep and lay our heads.

WHAT MAKES SENSE NOW

Shadow clouds paint gray sky
through autumn morning,

a brush stroke of one color
layered upon pockets of

bright yellow green leaves
never to turn brown or red

or gold, and the bike,
wet and uncared for, drips

rain from its handlebars
and morning holds its breath

until it can't any longer
and I take its exhale into

my own, letting space
between meaning hold my hand.

THE CHOICE TO TURN
(THE END OF IT)

The world is heavy and I
am heavy with disappointment
but not really, although
I have for most of my
life believed this, but
even now as I sit here
in the dark by the window,
watching morning peek open
one eye and then another like
a young child stretching its
sleepy limbs before it jumps
out of bed, tree branches once
laden with purple blooms
now bent with crispy red
golden leaves, eyelashes framing
the window panes as mist
puffs up from the house roof
into the great pine tree with
a branch broken from
yesterday's storm, I realize
I can't even conjure it any
more—this feeling disappointed
by all of it—my mistakes,
my dizzying efforts to remedy
what I felt I lacked,
my bad habits, my
pain as this burden
of being me—what I felt
and felt disappointed for
—has melted away, the

shroud disintegrated
with his touch, a crown
hard fought for I see
now upon my head.

Title Index

M

O

P

Q

R

FIRST LINE INDEX

Y

9 781594 981203